CW00383190

THE OFFICIAL
QUEENS PARK RANGERS
ANNUAL 2011

A Grange Publication

Written by Francis Atkinson & Ian Taylor
Designed by Colin Heggie

© 2010. Published by Grange Communications Ltd., Edinburgh, under licence from Queens Park Rangers Football Club.
Printed in the EU.

Photography © Backpage Images

ISBN: 978-1-907104-71-8

£7.99

CONTENTS

WELCOME

Welcome to The Official Queens Park Rangers Annual 2011

There's never a dull moment at Loftus Road – and the R's 2009/10 campaign proved to be no different.

From Adel Taarabt's stunning solo strike against Preston North End to 'that' astonishing 4-2 comeback win away at Derby County – the third consecutive match that QPR netted four times – we've got highlights aplenty in this annual so you can look back on another campaign full of action in W12.

And it doesn't stop there. Who can remember our exhilarating 4-1 victory at home to Reading in October when reduced to ten men in front of a partisan Loftus Road crowd? Or even a breathtaking 5-2 despatch of Barnsley only a month previously?

If all of that wasn't enough, we've got puzzles, quizzes, posters and much, much more!

Sit back, relax and read away to your hearts content!

Come on you R's!

Francis Atkinson & Ian Taylor

SEASON REVIEW

AUGUST

QPR 1, BLACKPOOL 1
Peter Ramage was the last-gasp hero for Rangers, as they came back from a goal down to draw with Blackpool on the opening day.

EXETER CITY 0, QPR 5
Wayne Routledge hit a classy treble to send the R's into round two of the League Cup thanks to a 5-0 win over the Grecians. Hogan Ephraim and Alessandro Pellicori were also on target.

PLYMOUTH ARGYLE 1, QPR 1
Rangers suffered more late heartbreak at Home Park, as a late Rory Fallon goal cancelled out Heidar Helguson's first half header.

BRISTOL CITY 1, QPR 0
A stunning Nicky Maynard goal 13 minutes from time condemned the R's to a first defeat of the campaign at Ashton Gate.

QPR 1, NOTTINGHAM FOREST 1
Rangers had to make do with a point, after Mikele Leigertwood's spectacular effort was cancelled out by David McGoldrick.

QPR 2, ACCRINGTON STANLEY 1
Hogan Ephraim and Wayne Routledge continued their scoring runs in the Carling Cup against Accrington Stanley, as they put Rangers into round three.

SCUNTHORPE UNITED 0, QPR 1
Adel Taarabt's first-half strike was enough for the R's, who picked up their first league win of the season at Glanford Park.

SEPTEMBER

QPR 1, PETERBOROUGH UNITED 1
Wayne Routledge was again on the scoresheet as QPR came from behind to take a share of the spoils against Peterborough at Loftus Road.

CARDIFF CITY 0, QPR 2
Arsenal loanee Jay Simpson was at the double, as Jim Magilton's men cruised to a comfortable victory against high-flying Cardiff City.

CHELSEA 1, QPR 0
Rangers bowed out of the Carling Cup with their heads held high, going down to a solitary Salomon Kalou effort at Stamford Bridge.

QPR 5, BARNSLEY 2
Akos Buzsaky was at the double, as Rangers eased to victory against Barnsley. Mikele Leigertwood, Jay Simpson and Ben Watson were also on the scoresheet.

NEWCASTLE UNITED 1, QPR 1
The R's fine form continued at St James' Park, as Jim Magilton's men claimed a deserved share of the spoils against table-topping Newcastle United, ending the Geordies' one-hundred per-cent home record.

OCTOBER
SWANSEA CITY 2, QPR 0
Nine-man Rangers succumbed to a 2-0 defeat at The Liberty Stadium. Skipper Martin Rowlands and fellow central midfielder Ben Watson both saw red for two bookable offences, before late goals from Mark Gower and Lee Trundle left the R's contemplating a first defeat in seven.

QPR 4, PRESTON NORTH END 0
Adel Taarabt bagged a goal of the season contender, as Rangers stylishly swept aside the Lilywhites at a raucous Loftus Road.

QPR 4, READING 1
Ben Watson saw red again, but Rangers ran riot in W12, scoring four goals for the second successive home match, with Akos Buzsaky amongst the scorers.

DERBY COUNTY 2, QPR 4
Rangers fought back from two goals down to thrash Derby County 4-2 in front of the live BBC TV cameras. Goals from Adel Taarabt, Gavin Mahon, Jay Simpson and Akos Buzsaky sealed the rout.

QPR 1, LEICESTER CITY 2
Rangers were unable to continue their recent fine form, as Leicester City took all three points in front of a season's best crowd at Loftus Road of 17,082.

NOVEMBER
QPR 1, CRYSTAL PALACE 1
Akos Buzsaky's fine goalscoring form continued, but Darren Ambrose's strike ensured honours ended even on Derby Day in W12.

SHEFFIELD WEDNESDAY 1, QPR 2
Kaspars Gorkss' late header clinched all three points for the R's, as Jim Magilton's side cemented their place in the top-six. ▶

DONCASTER ROVERS 2, QPR 0
Two goals in quick succession were enough for Doncaster Rovers, as they registered a maximum return against the R's.

QPR 2, COVENTRY CITY 2
The Hoops consolidated fifth spot in the second tier with a share of the spoils in a four goal thriller against Coventry.

DECEMBER

QPR 1, MIDDLESBROUGH 5
Rangers suffered only their second home league defeat of the season, as Gordon Strachan picked up his first win in charge of Middlesbrough.

WATFORD 3, QPR 1
Jim Magilton's reign ended, as the R's succumbed to a 3-1 defeat to Watford in front of the live Sky Sports TV cameras.

WEST BROMWICH ALBION 2, QPR 2
Simon Cox's 93rd minute strike denied the R's maximum points, as they came within seconds of claiming a magnificent victory over high-flying West Bromwich Albion under the guidance of Caretaker duo Steve Gallen and Marc Bircham.

QPR 1, SHEFFIELD UNITED 1
Honours were even between Rangers and Sheffield United, as Paul Hart started his reign as boss with a point in a tight encounter at Loftus Road.

QPR 2, BRISTOL CITY 1
Rangers played out their final fixture of the year at Loftus Road with a victory over promotion-chasing Bristol City, with goals from Jay Simpson and Mikele Leigertwood.

IPSWICH TOWN 3, QPR 0
Jon Stead was at the double, as Paul Hart suffered his first loss in charge of Rangers at Portman Road.

JANUARY

SHEFFIELD UNITED 1, QPR 1
Jay Simpson's tenth goal of the season was cancelled out by Richard Cresswell on the stroke of half time, as Rangers were forced to settle for a replay in the FA Cup third round.

QPR 2, SHEFFIELD UNITED 3
The R's late show proved immaterial in their FA Cup third round replay against the Blades, as United came out on top in an entertaining affair in W12.

BLACKPOOL 2, QPR 2
Mick Harford saw his men come from behind twice to earn a creditable draw against Ian Holloway's Blackpool at Bloomfield Road, with an audacious Adel Taarabt spot-kick and a stunning Matt Connolly volley sealing a share of the spoils.

NOTTINGHAM FOREST 5, QPR 0
Robert Earnshaw was at the double as Rangers suffered defeat against high-flying Nottingham Forest at the City Ground.

QPR 0, SCUNTHORPE UNITED 1
Garry Thompson's 74th minute strike was enough for Scunthorpe United, as they recorded back-to-back away wins with victory over the R's.

FEBRUARY

PETERBOROUGH UNITED 1, QPR 0
Mikele Leigertwood and Peter Ramage were both given their marching orders, as Rangers were undone by Aaron McLean's first-half strike for Peterborough United.

QPR 1, IPSWICH TOWN 2
Two first-half goals from David Norris and Daryl Murphy gave Ipswich Town their second away league win of the season, despite an improved second-half display from the R's.

COVENTRY CITY 1, QPR 0
Gary Deegan's tenth-minute strike proved to be enough for Coventry City against the Hoops in a lacklustre affair at The Ricoh Arena.

QPR 2, DONCASTER ROVERS 1
Antonio German and Jay Simpson were both on the scoresheet as the R's secured a maximum return against Doncaster Rovers at Loftus Road.

MIDDLESBROUGH 2, QPR 0
It was the tale of two penalties at Middlesbrough's Riverside Stadium - they were both awarded to the hosts, as QPR lost 2-0 in the North-East.

MARCH

QPR 3, WEST BROMWICH ALBION 1
Neil Warnock started his managerial reign at QPR in fine fashion with an excellent 3-1 victory over promotion-chasing West Bromwich Albion. Jay Simpson, Matt Connolly and Akos Buzsaky were all on target.

QPR 2, PLYMOUTH ARGYLE 0
Adel Taarabt and Damion Stewart were both on target as QPR collected three more vital points with victory over Plymouth Argyle at Loftus Road.

SHEFFIELD UNITED 1, QPR 1
Adel Taarabt bagged his seventh goal of the season as honours ended even between QPR and Sheffield United at Bramall Lane.

READING 1, QPR 0
Gylfi Sigurdsson's 85th minute penalty proved to be the difference between battling ten-man QPR and Reading, as the R's left the Madejski Stadium with nothing to show for a determined second-half display.

QPR 1, SWANSEA CITY 1
Antonio German came off the bench to grab a point for QPR in their entertaining clash with promotion-chasing Swansea City at Loftus Road.

QPR 1, DERBY COUNTY 1
Lee Cook's stunning low drive was not enough to give QPR victory against Derby.

PRESTON NORTH END 2, QPR 2
Rangers fought back from two goals down to snatch a deserved point against Preston North End, with Peter Ramage and Tamas Priskin in the goals. ▶

APRIL

QPR 1, SHEFFIELD WEDNESDAY 1
Alejandro Faurlin scored his first-ever goal for QPR, though Neil Warnock's dominant side had to settle for a point against Sheffield Wednesday at Loftus Road.

LEICESTER CITY 4, QPR 0
Martyn Waghorn capped a fine individual display with two goals as promotion contenders Leicester City sealed a comfortable win over QPR at the Walkers Stadium.

CRYSTAL PALACE 0, QPR 2
QPR edged closer to safety with a stylish win over London rivals Crystal Palace at Selhurst Park – as Neil Warnock returned to SE25 in some style.

QPR 0 CARDIFF CITY 1
Joe Ledley grabbed a late winner, as Cardiff City earned a win over QPR that guaranteed them a place in the top-six.

QPR 1, WATFORD 0
QPR claimed bragging rights with a 1-0 win over local neighbours Watford, thanks to Akos Buzsaky's first half spot-kick.

BARNSLEY 0, QPR 1
Mikele Leigertwood's unstoppable 20-yard drive sealed back-to-back wins on the road for QPR in their 1-0 win over Barnsley.

MAY

QPR 0, NEWCASTLE UNITED 1
Peter Ramage saw red against his former Club, as Peter Lovenkrands gave the Champions all three points on the final day of the season.

SPOT THE DIFFERENCE

There are six differences between the photographs, how many can you spot?

ANSWERS p60

FOUR OF THE BEST
ENGLAND INTERNATIONALS

STAN BOWLES

Stan was capped 5 times for England in the mid Seventies and scored 1 goal. The Rangers No. 10 made his England debut in 1974 against Portugal in Lisbon and was one of six new caps including QPR team mate Phil Parkes in goal. England started well and Bowles caught the eye but the match ended 0-0 and Sir Alf Ramsey was sacked afterwards. Stan Bowles' only goal for his country came in a 2-0 victory over Wales and he went on to make only 4 more appearances under Don Revie.

GERRY FRANCIS

Francis won 12 caps for England, between 1974 and 1976 and was captain for 8 of those matches, the first being against Switzerland. He scored 3 times for his country in total. His debut was a European qualifier vs. Czechoslovakia which England won with a rousing 3-0 score line. The most memorable match for the Rangers number 8 was surely the Home Championship clash at Wembley vs. Scotland when the men from the north of the border needed only a draw to take the title. A Gerry Francis inspired England ran out convincing 5-1 winners and the pick of the goals came as early as the 5th minute when Francis turned away from a challenge in the centre of the pitch, ran on and unleashed a dipping angled drive from fully 25 yards to set England on the way to victory.

TERRY FENWICK

gained 20 full England caps and appeared in the 1986 World Cup finals where he achieved the unenviable record of the most yellow cards, 3, in a single World Cup tournament. ▶

PAUL PARKER

Parker's prowess in defence for QPR was noticed by England coach Bobby Robson, who gave him his debut vs. Albania in 1989. After only gaining 5 caps he was selected at right back at the 1990 World Cup where he stayed, playing comfortably as England progressed to the semi-finals where they lost to Germany on penalties. Parker won 19 full England caps in total.

FIVE QPR PLAYERS CALLED UP FOR ENGLAND SQUAD... (below left to right) **DAVE THOMAS, STAN BOWLES GERRY FRANCIS, PHIL PARKES** and **IAN GILLARD**

ALEJANDRO FAURLIN

WORD SEARCH
FIRST TEAM

```
K A R Y R D T N A M R E G
N O W B C O N N O L L Y Z
N A G E L E F R N A S G S
A G R N L M G A D Y D S I
B U Z S A K Y W U N N G M
A N E H H M O O E R A E P
D O O W T R E G I E L N S
I N F U R P A Y T C W I O
R R R O H M R T G M O V N
R A B R A S T E W A R T K
T A A R A B T S S K R O G
M I A T N A L A B N O G C
M N E T E L G R P C A L E
```

CERNY	ROWLANDS	MAHON	BALANTA
RAMAGE	COOK	EPHRAIM	VINE
CONNOLLY	BUZSAKY	TAARABT	BORROWDALE
STEWART	FAURLIN	SIMPSON	HALL
LEIGERTWOOD	GORKSS	GERMAN	AGYEMANG

ANSWERS p60

MARTIN ROWLANDS

ON THE SPOT WITH...
PETER RAMAGE

FOOTBALL, FOOTBALL, FOOTBALL...

WHAT ARE YOUR EARLIEST MEMORIES OF FOOTBALL? Just playing with my mates after school. As soon as that school bell went we were straight out there, with jumpers for goalposts, and getting stuck in. We'd be out until the sun went down - they were great times.

WHEN DID YOU REALISE YOU WANTED TO BECOME A PROFESSIONAL FOOTBALLER? Probably soon after I joined Newcastle United, at the age of 11 or 12. Before that, I just played Sunday football, but when you're getting coached by professional coaches on a daily basis, you get the bug and want to be the very best you can be. That's when I realised I wanted to go on and make a living out of the game.

DID YOU EVER PLAY IN ANY OTHER POSITIONS WHEN YOU WERE GROWING UP? I was a striker when I went to Newcastle. I only moved back when we were playing a trial match and we had eight forwards and two defenders, and being stupid as I am, I volunteered to play at centre-half! I guess it worked out okay though.

WHO WAS YOUR FOOTBALL IDOL IN YOUR TEENS? Great question! I always looked up to Alan Shearer. His partnership with Les Ferdinand in that dream year for the Geordies was just unbelievable. Philippe Albert was also a huge favourite of mine. He was a cultured centre-half, with great vision and awareness, and no-one will ever forget that wonderful chip he scored against Manchester United in our five goal rout. That will go down forever in Geordie folklore. I've got to mention Peter Beardsley too - he's also a legend.

WHO IS YOUR BEST FRIEND IN FOOTBALL? Probably Michael Chopra. I've known him since I was nine years-old. We used to knock about with Andy Farrell, who's at York City now, and we're all still in touch to this day.

TEAM MATES...

WHO DO YOU ROOM WITH AND WHAT ARE THEIR MOST ANNOYING HABITS? I've roomed with a few of the lads to be fair, but most recently Gaz. He's a top bloke to be honest, but as any of the lads will tell you, he has this habit of letting out a random 'WOO!' at any given time!

WHO IS THE FUNNIEST PLAYER IN THE QPR SQUAD? I've got to agree with the others - Gav Mahon. He's always got a comeback. He's a chirpy so and so and is so quick-witted, you can never catch him out! Viney is funny too, but most of the time he's only funny because he's moaning!

WHICH OF YOUR TEAM-MATES WOULD YOU LEAST LIKE TO BE STUCK IN A LIFT WITH AND WHY? Damion Stewart, without any doubt. He's got the biggest backside I've ever seen or heard of and for that reason alone, he'd take up all the room! He'd also bore me to tears about Arsenal, Usain Bolt and anything else Jamaican.

WHICH PLAYER COMES IN FOR THE MOST STICK AROUND THE TRAINING GROUND AND WHY? It's poor Matteo Alberti. Sometimes I feel really sorry for him when he's get pelted by the lads, but most of the time he deserves it! If it's not the state of his hideous clothes, it's his big conk that comes in for stick!

TELL US SOMETHING WE DON'T KNOW ABOUT ONE OF YOUR TEAM-MATES. Mikele fancies himself as the next Jamie Oliver by all accounts! Apparently, him and his Mrs cook for each other once a week and he's meant to be seriously good in the kitchen.

AWAY FROM THE PITCH...

WHAT OTHER INTERESTS DO YOU HAVE AWAY FROM THE BEAUTIFUL GAME? I love my golf. I'm officially a 13 handicapper, but I'm playing to nine or 10 at the moment, so the lads keep calling me a bandit! I love a good film too, and I've got a ridiculously big DVD collection.

IF YOU COULD WIN ANY TROPHY IN THE WORLD OF SPORT, WHAT WOULD IT BE AND WHY? The World Cup is the pinnacle of world sport, no doubt about it. Every young sports-mad lad has dreamed about lifting the famous trophy at some stage, and I'm no different.

IF YOU COULD TRADE PLACES WITH ANY SINGLE SPORTSMAN FOR A DAY, WHO WOULD IT BE AND WHY? Tiger Woods. He's a phenomenon. The amount of majors he's won, in an era where there are so many other top golfers, is just amazing. He's got the mental strength to cope with anything that's thrown at him and he's an inspiration to amateur golfers around the world.

WHICH ONE THING COULD YOU NOT LIVE WITHOUT AND WHY? My family. My dad, mum and sister have always been so supportive to me throughout my career.

WHO IN HISTORY WOULD YOU MOST LIKE TO HAVE DINNER WITH AND WHY? I'd probably say Muhammad Ali. It would be intriguing to spend time with 'The Champ.'

ON THE SPOT WITH...
MATT CONNOLLY

FOOTBALL, FOOTBALL, FOOTBALL...

WHAT ARE YOUR EARLIEST MEMORIES OF FOOTBALL? Playing in the garden with my older brother, James.

WHEN DID YOU REALISE YOU WANTED TO BECOME A PROFESSIONAL FOOTBALLER? Probably when I was eight or nine years-old. I joined Arsenal when I was eight, so I guess it was around then that I started to wonder if I could become a professional.

DID YOU EVER PLAY IN ANY OTHER POSITIONS WHEN YOU WERE GROWING UP? Oh yeah, I played all over the place! I used to run all over the pitch chasing the ball. It was only when I went to Arsenal that a position was really sorted out for me, and I have played in defence ever since.

WHO WAS YOUR FOOTBALL IDOL IN YOUR TEENS? I'd have to say Zinedine Zidane. He was an absolute genius with the ball.

WHO IS YOUR BEST FRIEND IN FOOTBALL? I wouldn't say I have a best friend, to be honest. I'm fortunate to have a lot of good mates in the game. Here at QPR we've got a great bunch of lads.

TEAM MATES...

WHO DO YOU ROOM WITH AND WHAT ARE THEIR MOST ANNOYING HABITS? It recently changed. I now room with Gary Borrowdale. His worst habit? He's always trying to get me to gamble. Disgraceful behaviour!

WHO IS THE FUNNIEST PLAYER IN THE QPR SQUAD? Gavin Mahon, without doubt. His one-liners are brilliant. He's hilarious. I actually come to training with him and Mikele Leigerwood. It certainly makes the drive-in interesting.

WHICH OF YOUR TEAM-MATES WOULD YOU LEAST LIKE TO BE STUCK IN A LIFT WITH AND WHY? Angelo Balanta. I'd be on my own in there because he'd fall asleep straight away!

WHICH PLAYER COMES IN FOR THE MOST STICK AROUND THE TRAINING GROUND AND WHY? It's got to be Matteo Alberti – for his clothes and his nose!

TELL US SOMETHING WE DON'T KNOW ABOUT ONE OF YOUR TEAM-MATES. Gavin Mahon is a human sat-nav! If we get stuck in traffic on the way to training, he'll somehow discover a completely new route. He's unbelievable at it.

AWAY FROM THE PITCH...

WHAT OTHER INTERESTS DO YOU HAVE AWAY FROM THE BEAUTIFUL GAME? I enjoy boxing, snooker – and playing on the X-Box. I haven't played snooker for a while, but my highest break is 47, which isn't too bad.

IF YOU COULD WIN ANY TROPHY IN THE WORLD OF SPORT, WHAT WOULD IT BE AND WHY? I'd be happy with the World Cup or the Champions League. It would be such an incredible feeling to be part of a team that won one of those trophies.

IF YOU COULD TRADE PLACES WITH ANY SINGLE SPORTSMAN FOR A DAY, WHO WOULD IT BE AND WHY? It would be either Floyd Mayweather or Roger Federer. It would be great to experience being the world's best at an individual sport such as boxing or tennis. They are both unbelievable at what they do.

WHICH ONE THING COULD YOU NOT LIVE WITHOUT AND WHY? My family. They have been so supportive throughout my career and have always been there for me.

WHO IN HISTORY WOULD YOU MOST LIKE TO HAVE DINNER WITH AND WHY? Bobby Moore. It would be great to speak with him about football, and I'm sure I would learn so much just by talking with him.

PLAYER PROFILES

PETER RAMAGE
DEFENDER (22-11-83)

A versatile and committed defender, Peter Ramage joined QPR on a free transfer from Newcastle United in the summer of 2008.

The Ashington-born defender - who made 51 starts for his boyhood club prior to his move to Loftus Road - went from strength to strength in his first season with the R's, making 34 appearances in all competitions and consistently performing to a very high standard at right back.

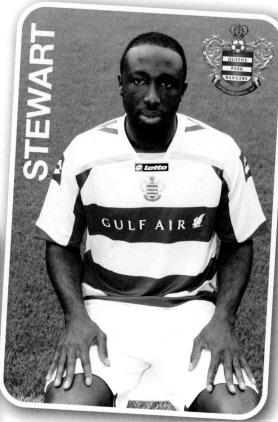

DAMION STEWART
DEFENDER (18-08-80)

Jamaican international Damion Stewart joined the R's in the summer of 2006.

After a steady, if unspectacular start, Stewart was a virtual ever-present in his first campaign in W12 and then went on to enjoy a productive second season at Loftus Road.

But it was the 2008/09 season - his third full campaign at this level - that saw Stewart's performances reach new heights, with the giant defender bagging four goals in all competitions, including the crucial winner against Aston Villa.

His displays at the heart of the Rangers back four secured him a notable end of season double, as he was named Supporters' Player and Player's Player of the Year.

GAVIN MAHON
MIDFIELDER (02-01-77)

Midfielder Gavin Mahon joined QPR in January 2008 from local rivals Watford.

A solid and reliable midfield general, Mahon - who skippered former club Watford to the Premiership during a five-year spell at Vicarage Road - made 40 appearances in all competitions last term.

During that spell, he also wore the skippers' armband, in the absence of regular Club Captain, Martin Rowlands.

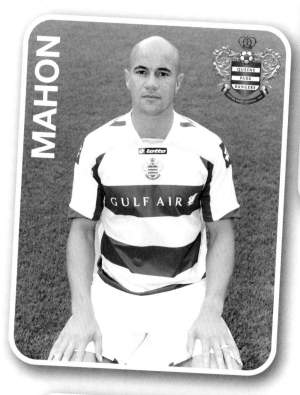

FITZ HALL
DEFENDER (20-12-80)

Fitz Hall penned a four-and-a-half year deal with Rangers at the start of the 2008 January transfer window.

The defender, who gained vast Premiership experience during spells at Wigan Athletic and Crystal Palace, suffered his fair share of injuries last term, and coupled with the emergence of Kaspars Gorkss, was restricted to just 27 appearances in all competitions.

MIKELE LEIGERTWOOD
MIDFIELDER (12-11-82)

Rangers completed the signing of no-nonsense midfielder Mikele Leigertwood on the final day of the 2007 summer transfer window.

The Sheffield United ace put pen to paper on a three-year deal, after the two Clubs agreed an undisclosed fee for his services.

Leigertwood went on to play a crucial role during his first season at Loftus Road, scoring a creditable five goals in 40 league appearances, and was a mainstay in the R's midfield last season too.

The midfielder made 46 appearances in all competitions, scoring two goals.

ROWAN VINE
STRIKER (21-09-82)

Queens Park Rangers completed the signing of Birmingham City front-man Rowan Vine in January 2008.

The experienced front-man signed a four-and-a-half year contract, after a successful loan period in W12.

Vine went on to bag three crucial goals in 15 appearances during his first season at Loftus Road, prior to sustaining a fractured leg during a freak training ground accident in early April.

That injury restricted his involvement last season, with the striker returning for the final few weeks of the campaign, scoring one goal in five appearances.

AKOS BUZSAKY
MIDFIELDER (07-05-82)

A player with outstanding individual ability, Akos Buzsaky made an immediate impact following his move to W12 from Plymouth Argyle. The Hungarian international scored six goals in his first 13 appearances, and ended the campaign with ten goals to his name.

Buzsaky's taste for the spectacular also saw him scoop the Kiyan Prince Goal of the Season award, but his first full season in W12 proved to be a frustrating one, with the talented ace notching just a solitary goal in his five league starts.

The midfielder suffered an Anterior Cruciate Ligament injury in the R's Carling Cup tie against Manchester United in November.

PATRICK AGYEMANG
STRIKER (29-09-80)

Patrick Agyemang joined QPR from Preston in January 2008 on a four-and-a-half year deal, after the two Clubs agreed an undisclosed fee for his services.

The Ghanaian international enjoyed a honeymoon period to remember for the R's, bagging eight goals in his first six league appearances.

Agyemang went on to score nine goals in all competitions, but injury struck last season.

The former Wimbledon man was restricted to just over 20 appearances in all competitions, scoring two goals, including one against his former club Preston on the final day of the season.

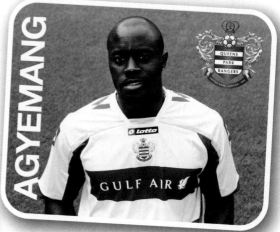

KASPARS GORKSS
DEFENDER (06-11-81)

Rangers ended their search for a centre half with the capture of Kaspars Gorkss in July 2008.

The Latvian international put pen to paper on a three year deal, after the R's agreed an undisclosed fee with Blackpool for his services.

And the giant defender - after a mixed start to life in W12 - went on to enjoy a profitable maiden season at Loftus Road, making 35 appearances in all competitions, and finishing runner-up in both the Player's Player and Supporters' Player of the Year awards.

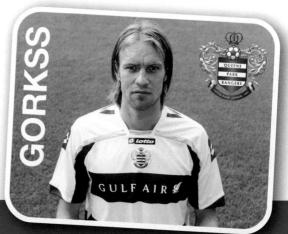

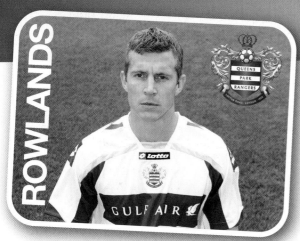

MARTIN ROWLANDS
MIDFIELDER (08-02-79)

Hammersmith-born midfielder Martin Rowlands joined Rangers in July 2003 on a free transfer from local rivals Brentford.

An outstanding 2007/08 campaign saw the midfielder named Player's Player of the Year and after a four-year absence from the international fold, Rowlands was recalled to the full Republic of Ireland squad under new Eire boss Giovanni Trapattoni.

But his 2008/09 campaign failed to hit such heights, with an Anterior Cruciate Ligament injury – sustained against Derby County in January - ruling him out for the season.

However, he still featured in the end of season awards, with his sublime strike against Wolverhampton Wanderers sealing the coveted Kiyan Prince Goal of the Season crown.

MATTHEW CONNOLLY
DEFENDER (24-09-87)

Matthew Connolly penned a three-and-a-half year deal with the R's in January 2008.
A product of the successful Arsenal academy, Connolly went on to make 21 appearances in all competitions for Rangers in his first six months at the Club.

Those displays led to a deserved call up to Stuart Pearce's England Under-21 squad and the versatile defender has excelled ever since.

Connolly made 39 appearances for the R's in the 2008/09 term, and was rightly named Supporters' Young Player of the Year.

LEE COOK
MIDFIELDER (03-08-82)

R's fans favourite Lee Cook rejoined Rangers on loan from Fulham in August 2008.
The left sided midfielder, who joined the Cottagers just 12 months earlier, was named both Player's Player and Supporter's Player of the Year prior to his departure to the West London outfit.

But an injury-interrupted spell at Craven Cottage eventually led to his return to W12, and after making his loan deal permanent in January 2009, Cook went on to make 38 appearances in all competitions last term and scored a stunning free-kick against Charlton Athletic on Boxing Day.

ANGELO BALANTA
FORWARD (01-07-90)

Teenage striker Angelo Balanta put pen-to-paper on his first professional contract with the R's in January 2008.

The teenage Colombian, who made three First Team appearances in his time as an Under-18 player, inked a deal that keeps him at the Club until the summer of 2010.

After scoring in the R's Carling Cup victory against Swindon Town at the start of the 2008/09 season, Balanta excelled during a loan spell at Wycombe Wanderers, before returning to W12 for the final few months of the campaign.

RADEK CERNY
GOALKEEPER (18-02-74)

Goalkeeper Radek Cerny joined the R's in the summer of 2008.

The former Tottenham Hotspur and Slavia Prague stopper arrived in W12 with a terrific track record and duly went on to make the number one jersey his own.

Cerny was a mainstay in the R's side throughout the 2008/09 campaign, making 47 appearances in all competitions, and inspiring Rangers to one of the best defensive records in the Championship.

JAY SIMPSON
STRIKER (01-12-88)

Rangers swooped to complete the loan signing of Jay Simpson just five days prior to the summer transfer window slamming shut. The 20 year-old, who joined Arsenal at the tender age of nine, penned a season-long loan deal in W12.

Simpson - who has represented England at Under-17 and Under-18 level - made history when he became the first ever player to score a hat-trick at The Emirates Stadium, for Arsenal's Under-18 side in a 3-2 FA Youth Cup win against Cardiff City.

HOGAN EPHRAIM
MIDFIELDER (31-03-88)

After a successful loan spell in W12, winger Hogan Ephraim signed a three-and-a-half year contract with QPR in January 2008.

The diminutive winger made 30 appearances in all competitions in 2007/08, scoring two goals and proved what a valuable, versatile asset he is to the R's side again last term.

The midfielder scored a stunning third goal in our 3-0 demolition of Blackpool, as the former England Youth product excelled in a more central role.

HEIDAR HELGUSON
STRIKER (22-08-77)

QPR rescued Iceland international Helguson from Bolton Wanderers after the former Watford man fell out of favour under then-Manager Gary Megson.

Initially signed on a loan deal, he made the move to W12 permanent as soon as the transfer window opened in January 2009.

Three goals in seven appearances indicated a man relieved to be back playing, and he has added a new dimension to the Rangers attack with tireless work rate and phenomenal aerial prowess.

Helguson went on to finish the campaign with five goals in 21 appearances in all competitions.

ALEJANDRO FAURLIN
MIDFIELDER (09-08-86)

Argentine midfielder Alejandro Faurlin became Jim Magilton's first signing at QPR, when he penned a three year deal at Loftus Road, in a deal worth £3.5 million.

Faurlin, who made 34 appearances last year for the Argentine club Instituto, has a sweet left foot and is highly rated in his homeland.

Faurlin made an immediate impact in pre-season, impressing in a central midfield berth for Magilton's men.

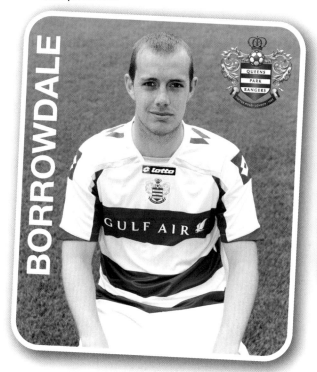

GARY BORROWDALE
DEFENDER (16-07-85)

Former England Under-21 defender Gary Borrowdale joined the R's from Coventry City in January 2009.

However, his first six months in W12 proved to be frustrating, with the defender spending most of that time on loan at League One outfit Brighton & Hove Albion.

ADEL TAARABT
Midfielder (24-05-89)

Rangers completed the season-long loan signing of Tottenham Hotspur midfielder Adel Taarabt just a fortnight prior to the start of the 2009/10 campaign.

The Moroccan international spent three months of the previous campaign on loan, and made a stunning impact, turning in one superlative display after another.

And he continued that during pre-season, scoring a quite stupendous individual goal in the 3-0 rout of Southampton.

2010/11 KIT

The new QPR home strip features the iconic Blue and White Hoops, as well as a new thin red piping, harping back to the popular Guinness jersey from the early 1980s.

R'S ACE Akos Buzsaky, who modeled the kit at our official launch, is a huge advocate of the new strip, commenting: "It's very nice - I really like the way it looks. Hopefully the fans will like it as much as we do.

"The most important thing is that it is a successful kit, and that is down to us."

Fellow midfielder Lee Cook added: "I always like it when the new kit comes out, and this one is really smart.

"They've brought the red bit back, and the badge is now on the side which looks really good. The whole kit is a lot better."

The new home jersey retains the traditional hoops in reflex blue and white, but this year, the Lotto Sport Italia logo is positioned on the left side of the jersey, with the QPR Club Crest situated on the right. The new Gulf Air logo is once again placed within the blue hoops, matching the signage around Loftus Road.

OUR ARGENTINIAN ACE

Ian Taylor takes a look back at Alejandro Faurlin's meteoric rise to stardom during his first 12 months at Loftus Road, which culminated in his scooping the prestigious Supporter's Player of the Year and Player's Player of the Year accolades at the end of the 2009/10 campaign...

OSVALDO ARDILES and Ricky Villa did it to devastating effect at Tottenham Hotspur in the late-Seventies, but very few Argentinean footballers have been able to settle into life on these shores quite as easily as Alejandro Faurlin.

It was in early July 2009, in pre-season training, that I got my first glimpse of the then 22 year-old in action.

Quiet yet confident, Faurlin appeared to be in his comfort zone at the R's training ground, quickly asserting his class on proceedings and comfortably mixing with his team-mates, most notably Akos Buzsaky and Matteo Alberti, whose ability to speak the Portuguese and Spanish language respectively built bridges in the opening few weeks.

Such was Faurlin's impact, that then Manager Jim Magilton

wasted no time in making his trial move permanent, with the R's agreeing a record fee with Instituto for his services on a three year deal.

The rest is history – with Faurlin making one giant stride after another, on his way to enjoying what can only be described as a memorable maiden season in W12.

Highlights aplenty – including that all so important first goal in QPR colours against Sheffield Wednesday in April – Faurlin attributes his fantastic first season to the 'family feel' of the Club, commenting: "The QPR fans are just wonderful, they have been amazing," he adds.

"The Club is perfect, it is like my home. I feel very comfortable here.

"For the fans, I want to say a big thank you because I feel very positive. And I always want more. I want progress, progress, progress. I am very happy, and thank you so much for your support.

"But we all want more. For me, it was a good first season, but we want to make forward strides year after year."

Like his predecessors before him, Neil Warnock clearly rates Faurlin as a player, and it is with bated breath that R's fans await the next chapter of the Argentinian ace's career in W12.

If his awards double at the end-of-season showcase last May is anything to go by, the sky really is the limit for the R's midfield lynchpin, who appears to have the world of football at his ever-so talented feet. ▶

PLAYER OF THE YEAR AWARDS 2009/10 ROLL OF HONOUR

SUPPORTERS' PLAYER OF THE YEAR
(SPONSORED BY MARSAFE ENVIRONMENTAL SERVICES):
ALEJANDRO FAURLIN

SUPPORTERS' PLAYER OF THE YEAR RUNNER-UP
(SPONSORED BY STAN JAMES):
KASPARS GORKSS

PLAYERS' PLAYER OF THE YEAR
(SPONSORED BY LOTTO TEAM WEAR):
ALEJANDRO FAURLIN

SUPPORTERS' YOUNG PLAYER OF THE YEAR
(SPONSORED BY BIG YELLOW SELF STORAGE):
ADEL TAARABT

KIYAN PRINCE GOAL OF THE SEASON
(SPONSORED BY EMS INTERNET):
ADEL TAARABT (v PRESTON NORTH END)

SUPPORTER OF THE YEAR (sponsored by QPR Card):
LEE BUTLER

QPR COMMUNITY AWARD (sponsored by Sharon Dyer):
OMAR SALIH

MIKELE LEIGERTWOOD

SPARK

SPOT THE BALL

Study the picture below closely, then use your skill to spot where you think the ball might be?

ANSWERS p60

SIX OF THE BEST GOALS 2009/10

Despite a topsy-turvy season, the R's were involved in some truly mouth-watering encounters last term – and scored some quite remarkable goals!
We've selected 'Six of the Best' and you can make your own mind up as to which one you believe is the pick of the bunch.

GOAL 1

1 ADEL TAARABT
v PRESTON NORTH END (H)

ADEL TAARABT was arguably one of the brightest sparks for QPR last season, producing one superb performance after another in an attacking role.

But his best moment of the entire campaign arrived against the Lilywhites, when – having picked up possession deep inside his own half – he left four defenders trailing in his wake, one with an audacious nut-meg, before setting himself to shoot 25 yards from goal.

The rest was pure poetry in motion, as his stunning right foot curler arched into the roof of the net, giving PNE stopper Andy Lonergan absolutely no chance.

GOAL 2

2 MATT CONNOLLY
v BLACKPOOL (A)

MATT CONNOLLY enhanced his ever growing reputation with a quite stunning strike in our 2-2 draw at Bloomfield Road – and in doing so, opened his account for the R's.

The former Arsenal defender ensured the R's left the seaside with a share of the spoils, thanks to a goal that was fit to grace any stadium in the world.

Arriving on to a loose ball, Connolly took one touch to set himself before blasting home a sensational looping 25-yard volley that left Pool goalkeeper Paul Rachubka absolutely motionless.

3 GAVIN MAHON
v DERBY COUNTY (A)

TEAM GOALS often get overlooked when it comes to picking the best strikes of the season, but this one is right up there!

Just moments into the second half – and with the R's trailing 2-1 – Rangers conjured a goal right out of the top drawer, with the outstanding Mahon finishing in style.

Breaking from deep, Wayne Routledge proved to be the catalyst, and when Gary Borrowdale and Alejandro Faurlin quickly exchanged passes, the ball fell at the feet of Adel Taarabt.

He in turn picked out the on-rushing Routledge, who had both the guile and the

vision to pick out the marauding Mahon, who arrived bang on cue to draw the R's level from the edge of the six-yard box.

4 MIKELE LEIGERTWOOD
v BARNSLEY (A)

TO QUOTE Neil Warnock, 'Mikele doesn't get many, but when he does it's normally an absolute cracker!' – and this was certainly no exception.

With Rangers totally orchestrating proceedings in what was effectively an end-of-season dead-rubber at Oakwell, Leigertwood gave the travelling R's faithful something to shout about – and how!

With very little space on the edge of the Tykes box, the Hoops stand-in skipper let fly with a fearsome left-footed drive that cannoned in off the bar.

5 JAY SIMPSON
v READING (H)

JAY SIMPSON topped the R's goalscoring charts – thanks in no small part to the contribution of Wayne Routledge, who again played provider for this peach of a team goal against Reading.

It took just 13 seconds for the R's to spring from defence to attack, with Radek Cerny, Alejandro Faurlin and Akos Buzsaky all playing their part, before the ball eventually fell to the nippy Routledge.

His cross to the far post was simply divine and Simpson did the rest, thrashing home an unstoppable close-range volley that inspired the R's to a four goal rout of the Royals.

6 AKOS BUZSAKY
v BARNSLEY (H)

AKOS BUZSAKY rarely nets anything other than a contender for Goal of the Season and this strike against Barnsley was right up there with the best of them.

On a bright September Saturday in West London, the Magical Magyar spotted Tykes custodian David Preece off his line and picked his spot with a delightful curling effort that looped into the back of the net.

It was Buzsaky's second goal of the afternoon and inspired Rangers to a 5-2 victory over Mark Robins' men.

PETER RAMAGE

CROSS WORD

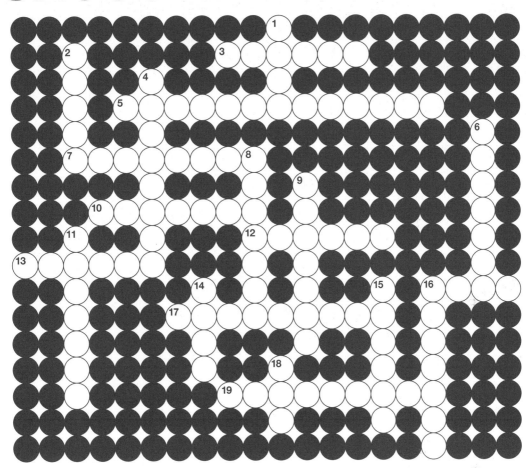

ACROSS

3 First name of scorer of our last goal of the season? (6)

5 Which club inflicted QPR's biggest defeat at home? (13)

7 Surname of midfielder injured while on international duty against Montenegro? (8)

10 Scottish international who joined on a short term contract last season? (7)

12 Midfielder who got sent off on his return from a red card? (6)

13 Defender from Latvia? (6)

16 First name of defender who made 12 starts for Rangers last season? (4)

17 Scored a hat-trick against Exeter in the Carling Cup? (9)

19 Premier league-bound team got a 1-1 draw at Loftus Road on the opening day of the 09/10 season? (9)

DOWN

1 First name of player who scored a free-kick against Reading? (4)

2 First name of defender who scored the first QPR goal of the season? (5)

4 Tommy, the former R's player who returned to us on loan for part of the season? (8)

6 Player voted scoring the goal of the season? (7)

8 Surname of player injured within 30 seconds at Crystal Palace? (7)

9 First name of defender who scored the 2nd R's goal away to Blackpool? (7)

11 Surname of striker who came to the R's from Ipswich? (7)

14 Surname of squad number 17? (4)

15 Goalkeeper on loan from Manchester United was who? (6)

16 The Superhoops Player of the Season? (7)

18 First name of striker who got on the score sheet twice at Cardiff? (3)

ANSWERS p61

43

BETWEEN THE STICKS

CHRIS DAY joined QPR in the summer of 2001 on a free transfer from Watford and made his debut in a 1-0 victory over Stoke. He overcame a broken leg and forced his way back into the side which eventually lost 1-0 in the 2nd Division play-off final to Cardiff. He was instrumental in the teams great defensive record the season after and kept an amazing 16 clean sheets in the first 6 months of the season. However injury robbed him of his finest hour again as Lee Camp came in to cover for him in the latter stages and held his place as Rangers won at Hillsborough to secure that famous promotion. Day eventually left in 2005 after making 100 appearances.

DAVID SEAMAN came to prominence as the QPR keeper between 1986 and 1990 making 141 appearances for the R's and gaining his first full England cap in a friendly against Saudi Arabia in November 1988 under Bobby Robson. Seaman went on to make 75 appearances for England during an illustrious career which was predominately spent at Arsenal.

JAN STEJSKAL was born on 15 January 1962 and was capped 31 times for his country Czechoslovakia (later the Czech Republic) participating in the 1990 world cup. He signed for QPR in 1990 and was one of only 13 foreign players to play on the opening weekend of the FA Premier league. Stejskal was a tall, commanding goalkeeper and once he had

overcome his language difficulties went on to become one of QPR's finest keepers. After 107 appearances in West London, the giant 6ft 6in stopper returned home to SK Slavia Praha.

PETER HUCKER joined QPR as a schoolboy in December 1974 and turned professional in 1977 making his league debut vs. Shrewsbury in 1981. He had played very few first team games prior to a 3rd round cup tie at Loftus Road in 1982 vs. Middlesbrough but first-choice keeper John Burridge was injured and Hucker grabbed his chance with a series of impressive displays, retaining his place throughout that season. This culminated in the Ranger No. 1 being awarded 'Man of the Match' in the FA Cup final vs. Tottenham despite the fact that he was injured. Rangers went on to lose the replay 1-0 (penalty) but Hucker played a key role the following season as the boys from W12 stormed to the 2nd Division title and followed that up by finishing as London's top club in the First Division (now the Premier league) and qualified for Europe. Terry Venables left the club in 1984 and like many others Hucker's form suffered and he lost his place to Paul Barron in 1985/86 season, eventually he moved to Oxford United in February 1987. Peter played 154 league games for QPR.

PETER SPRINGETT (not pictured) played for QPR on 137 occasions, his debut being versus Peterborough United in 1963. He was part of the QPR team that not only won the League Cup in 1967, coming from behind against 1st Division West Brom to win 3-2, but also that took the 3rd Division championship in the same season. Peter moved to Sheffield Wednesday in 1967 in a unique swap deal for his brother, England international, Ron.

RON SPRINGETT (pictured left). Ron started his career at QPR before moving to Sheffield Wednesday for £10,000. After 304 appearances for the Owls he returned to W12 in May 1967 in that swap deal. He was first-choice England stopper at the 1962 World Cup in Chile and was also part of the triumphant 1966 World Cup winning squad.

THE BIG QUIZ

1 Who scored QPR's equaliser on the opening day of the 2009/10 campaign against Blackpool?

2 Which former QPR midfielder bagged a hat-trick in our Carling Cup thrashing of Exeter City?

3 Who did the R's play in their first away League game of the season?

4 At which ground did Rangers suffer their first away defeat of the campaign?

5 Which Italian summer signing made his full debut against Nottingham Forest in mid August?

6 Who scored QPR's winner against Scunthorpe United at Glanford Park?

7 Who bagged a brace in our 2-0 win against Cardiff City?

8 Which goalkeeper made his first start for the R's against Chelsea in the Carling Cup third round?

9 From which Club did QPR sign midfielder Ben Watson on loan?

10 How many goals did QPR score in our three fixtures against Preston North End, Reading and Derby County in October?

11 Who bagged QPR's winner at Sheffield Wednesday, which lifted the R's into fourth place in the Championship table?

12 Tommy Williams joined QPR on loan from which Club in November?

13 By what scoreline did Middlesbrough beat Rangers at Loftus Road at the start of December?

14 Who joined QPR as Paul Hart's number two at the end of 2009?

15 Which defender bagged his first goal in the Blue and White Hoops with a contender for goal of the season against Blackpool?

16 Which two players saw red in our 1-0 defeat to Peterborough United at the start of February?

17 Neil Warnock's reign began with a 3-1 win against West Bromwich Albion – but who scored the R's all-important third goal in that victory?

18 Which QPR loanee was adjudged to have committed a foul which led to the award of a penalty in the R's 1-0 defeat at Reading?

19 Who scored the R's only goal of the game in our final victory of the campaign versus Barnsley at Oakwell?

20 Who scored the final goal of the season at Loftus Road, as Newcastle United ran out 1-0 winners in W12?

ANSWERS p61

KASPARS GORKSS

AKOS BUZSAKY

NUMBERS UP

1882 The year Queens Park Rangers Football Club was formed

13th The R's final League position at the end of the 2009/10 Coca Cola Championship campaign

10 The squad number worn by the Magical Magyar, Akos Buzsaky

44.1% The win percentage enjoyed by Gordon Jago between 1971 and 1974

1967 The year the R's scooped the League Cup, with victory over West Bromwich Albion

39 years **352** days The age of Ray Wilkins when he became the oldest ever player to represent the Club

52 The number of Northern Ireland caps won by former R's centre-back Alan McDonald

6,000,000 The record transfer fee received from Newcastle United for Les Ferdinand in June 1995

44 The number of goals scored by Rodney Marsh in the 1966/67 campaign

35,353 The Club's record attendance against Leeds United in April 1974

3,500,000 The record transfer fee paid to Instituto for Alejandro Faurlin in the summer of 2009

15 years **275** days The age of Frank Sibley when he became the youngest ever player to represent QPR

6 Mikele Leigertwood's current squad number

1st Newcastle United (Champions)
The Magpies
St James' Park
Chris Hughton
Home L 1-0
Away D 1-1

2nd West Bromwich Albion (Runners-up)
The Baggies
The Hawthorns
Roberto Di Matteo
Home W 3-1
Away D 2-2

3rd Nottingham Forest
The Reds
The City Ground
Billy Davies
Home D 1-1
Away L 5-0

4th Cardiff City
The Bluebirds
Cardiff City Stadium
Dave Jones
Home L 1-0
Away W 2-0

5th Leicester City
The Foxes
Walkers Stadium
Nigel Pearson
Home L 2-1
Away L 4-0

6th Blackpool (Promoted)
The Seasiders
Bloomfield Road
Ian Holloway
Home D 1-1
Away D 2-2

7th Swansea City
The Swans
Liberty Stadium
Paulo Sousa
Home D 1-1
Away L 2-0

8th Sheffield United
The Blades
Bramall Lane
Kevin Blackwell
Home D 1-1
Away D 1-1

AROUND THE CHAMPIONSHIP GROUNDS 2009/10

9th Reading
The Royals
Madejski Stadium
Brian McDermott
Home W 4-1
Away L 1-0

10th Bristol City
The Robins
Ashton Gate
Steve Coppell
Home W 2-1
Away L 1-0

11th Middlesbrough
Boro'
Riverside Stadium
Gordon Strachan
Home L 5-1
Away L 2-0

12th Doncaster Rovers
Rovers
Keepmoat Stadium
Sean O'Driscoll
Home W 2-1
Away L 2-0

13th QPR
Rangers
Loftus Road
Neil Warnock
Home P23, W8, D9, L6
Away P23, W6, D6, L11

14th Derby County
The Rams
Pride Park
Nigel Clough
Home D 1-1
Away W 4-2

15th Ipswich Town
Tractor Boys
Portman Road
Roy Keane
Home L 2-1
Away L 3-0

16th Watford
Hornets
Vicarage Road
Malky Mackay
Home W 1-0
Away L 3-1

17th Preston North End
Lilywhites
Deepdale
Darren Ferguson
Home W 4-0
Away D 2-2

18th Barnsley
The Tykes
Oakwell
Mark Robins
Home W 5-2
Away W 1-0

19th Coventry City
Sky Blues
The Ricoh Arena
Aidy Bothroyd
Home D 2-2
Away L 1-0

20th Scunthorpe United
The Iron
Glanford Park
Nigel Adkins
Home L 1-0
Away W 1-0

21st Crystal Palace
The Eagles
Selhurst Park
Paul Hart
Home D 1-1
Away W 2-0

22nd Sheffield Wednesday (relegated)
The Owls
Hillsborough
Alan Irvine
Home D 1-1
Away W 2-1

23rd Plymouth Argyle (relegated)
The Pilgrims
Home Park
Paul Mariner
Home W 2-0
Away D 1-1

24th Peterborough United (relegated)
The Posh
London Road
Gary Johnson
Home D 1-1
Away L 1-0

THE CHAMPIONSHIP NEWCOMERS
FROM THE PREMIER LEAGUE...

Burnley
The Clarets
Turf Moor
Brian Laws
Capacity 22,546

Hull City
The Tigers
The KC Stadium
Iain Dowie
Capacity 25,404

Portsmouth
Pompey
Fratton Park
Position Vacant
Capacity 20,688

FROM LEAGUE ONE...

Norwich City
The Canaries
Carrow Road
Paul Lambert
Capacity 26,034

Leeds United
Whites
Elland Road
Simon Grayson
Capacity 39,460

Millwall
Lions
The Den
Kenny Jackett
Capacity 20,146

FITZ HALL

HOGAN EPHRAIM

GETTING SHIRTY

You probably know their Manager's, players and Club crests – but do you know these Championship teams' home kits?

ANSWERS p61

QUIZ ANSWERS

p13 SPOT THE DIFFERENCE

p20 WORD SEARCH

```
K A R Y R D T N A M R E G
N O W B C O N N O L L Y Z
N A G E L E F R N A S G S
A G R N L M G A D Y D S I
B U Z S A K Y W U N N G M
A N E H H M O O E R A E P
D O O W T R E G I E L N S
I N F U R P A Y T C W I O
R R R O H M R T G M O V N
R A B R A S T E W A R T K
T A A R A B T S S K R O G
M I A T N A L A B N O G C
M N E T E L G R P C A L E
```

p37 SPOT THE BALL

p43 CROSS WORD

```
                A
            M I K E L E
   P        O
   E        M I D D L E S B R O U G H
   T   W    T                     T
   E   I    T   M                 A
   R O W L A N D S                A
       L    R   A                 R
   P   Q U A S H I E              A
   R   I    R   W A T S O N       B
   G O R K S S  T   H       H  F I T Z
   I   I    C R     E A     A  A
   S        R O U T L E D G E    U
   K        O    D   W     A     R
   I        O          J   T     I
   N        K          A         N
            B L A C K P O O L
                       J
                       Y
```

p54 THE BIG QUIZ

1   PETER RAMAGE
2   WAYNE ROUTLEDGE
3   PLYMOUTH ARGYLE
4   ASHTON GATE
5   ALESSANDRO PELLICORI
6   ADEL TAARABT
7   JAY SIMPSON
8   TOM HEATON
9   WIGAN ATHLETIC
10 12
11 KASPARS GORKSS
12 PETERBOROUGH UNITED
13 5-1
14 MICK HARFORD
15 MATTHEW CONNOLLY
16 PETER RAMAGE &
    MIKELE LEIGERTWOOD
17 AKOS BUZSAKY
18 MATT HILL
19 MIKELE LEIGERTWOOD
20 PETER LOVENKRANDS

p59 GETTING SHIRTY

A   MIDDLESBROUGH
B   PRESTON NORTH END
C   SWANSEA CITY
D   WATFORD
E   BRISTOL CITY

p62 WHERE'S SPARK?